Sloatsburg Public Library
1 Liberty Rock Rd.
Sloatsburg, NY 10974

7/12

DEMCO

For Girls!

Happy
and
Healthy

Deborah
Chancellor

QEB

QEB Publishing

Editor: Mandy Archer
Designer: Nikki Kenwood
Illustrator: Jessica Secheret

First published in the United States in 2011 by
QEB Publishing. Inc.
3 Wrigley, Suite A
Irvine, CA 92618

www.qed-publishing.co.uk

Library of Congress Cataloging-in-Publication Data

Chancellor, Deborah.
 Happy and healthy / Deborah Chancellor.
    p. cm. -- (For girls!)
 Includes index.
 Summary: "This guide for girls gives advice on how to keep healthy, including exercise and
keeping fit, creative cooking, skin and hair care, healthy foods, and sports"--Provided by publisher.
 ISBN 978-1-60992-104-0 (library binding)
1. Girls--Life skills guides--Juvenile literature. 2. Girls--Health and hygiene--Juvenile literature.
3. Beauty, Personal--Juvenile literature. I. Title.
 HQ777.C524 2012
 646.7`046--dc22

                            2011006913

ISBN 978 1 60992 104 0

Printed in China

Picture credits
(t=top, b=bottom, l=left, r=right, c=center, fc=front cover)
Shutterstock 4 blue67design and azzzya (spot art), 4l NatUlrich,
4r Alena Ozerova, 4b heromen30, 5l Elena Elisseeva, 5bc Anke van Wyk, 6r Diana Olsevska,
6 Stephanie Lirette (spot art), 6 khz (spot art), 7t Zand, 7l Alena Ozerova, 7b NatUlrich, 8
PILart (spot art), 8t Vibrant Image Studio, 8bl Angela Jones, 8br eAlisa, 9c Martin Mette, 9b
Pete Saloutos, 10tl Amenhotepov, 10b Alexander Kalina, 11t Stawek, 11cl Olha Ukhal, 11cr
FreeSoulProduction, 12 nata_danilenko (spot art), 12 Lota (spot art), 12c Yuri Arcurs,12b ifong,
13l Pilgrim Artworks, 13r Galayko Sergey,
13r Monkey Business Images, 13bl Kraska, 14t beboy, 14c Stephen Aaron Rees, 14b Monkey
Business Images, 15c LittleRambo, 16 notkoo (spot art), 16t Rick P Lewis, 16b Booka, 17c
Takra, 17b Gina Sanders, 18r Rakov Studio, 19t Yuri Arcurs, 19c Callahan, 19 Triling Studio
LTd. (spot art), 20b zeljkosantrac, 20r zsooofija, 21tl U.P.images_vector, 21tr ildogesto, 21cl
Shmeliova Natalia, 21br volod, 22tr Aleksandr Markin, 23r Ardelean Andreea, 23cl Yuri Arcurs,
23br maraga, 24t Monkey Business Images, 24c Monkey Business Images, 25t Liliya Kulianionak,
25b Fernando Blanco Calzada, 26t Pushkin, 26l Petro Feketa, 26lc Jiri Hera, 27 Lavanda and
nata_danilenko (spot art), 27c Stavklem & Roman Kholodov,
27b michaeljung, 28t Monkey Business Images, 29t sonia.eps. **Photolibrary** 15t Stockbrokerextra
Images.

Contents

Get in Shape!

You only have one body—so it's up to you to take care of it. Getting active is the best way to keep yourself happy and healthy. Just go for it!

Couch Potato

Do you watch too much television? Make a note each day of how long you sit in front of the TV. After a week, look back at how many hours you spent—is it time to cut back and do something more active instead?

Computer Crazy?

Surfing the web and playing computer games doesn't give your muscles much of a workout! Take regular breaks and listen to your mom or dad if they nag you to hop up and do something else!

Take It Outside!

Fix a time to meet your friends after school—why not use up some energy skating around the park or shooting hoops at the neighborhood basketball court? Don't forget to tell someone at home where you're going and when you'll be back.

Stretch Your Legs

Look for new ways to make exercise part of your everyday life. If you have an older brother or sister, ask them to walk to school with you instead of getting a ride. If you live too far away, ask your parents to stop the car nearby and walk the rest of the way.

Like Your Bike

Cycling is a super-quick way to get around! If you are not confident at riding yet, go out with your mom or dad a few times first. Always wear a helmet and choose routes that are safe for cycling.

Road Safety

If you are walking with friends or riding your bikes, be careful near busy roads. If you are cycling, wear a helmet and make sure that you can be easily seen in the dark.

Move It!

Why not...?
- scooter to the store
- jog around the block
- ban elevators and take the stairs
- powerwalk the dog
- skateboard down the sidewalk

Indoor Play

Weather not so good? There are still hundreds of indoor sports you can enjoy! Get ready to challenge yourself and share lots of giggles at the same time...

Get Together

If you are shy and find it hard to make friends, join a sports club. There are clubs for every sport you can think of. You could even have some lessons first to help build your confidence.

Fantastic Gymnastics

Gymnastics is a cool indoor sport for girls. You can go to gym classes, and there are a lot of awards to work for as you improve your skills.

Sky-high

Trampolining keeps you fit and uses up loads of energy. The trick to good bouncing is to get into a rhythm! Learn some awesome moves, then make up your own routine.

Gym Basics

Can you master all six?

1. forward roll
2. handstand
3. backward roll
4. cartwheel
5. headstand
6. handspring

Super Skating

Ice-skating is an Olympic sport that can be really competitive. It takes years of hard work to become an ice-skating champ, but there's a lot of fun to be had just gliding around your local rink!

Dance Studio

Moving to music will have you working up a sweat in no time! There are so many ways to do it, too. Ballet, tap, jazz, street, Latin, and ballroom are all different types of dancing.

Look Out!

Martial arts such as judo, jujitsu, and karate can help keep you both fit and safe. The skills you learn are handy for self-defense. One of the first things you will be taught is how to fall without hurting yourself.

Splash Time

If you can't swim, take the plunge and learn! If you're already pool-confident, work on improving your technique so you speed up in the water.

Splashing Sports

Give these wicked water sports a try!

- surfing
- canoeing
- waterskiing
- snorkeling
- windsurfing
- rowing

Water Baby

Don't worry if all your buddies can swim, but you can't. It's never too late to learn! Sign up for beginner's lessons. Some pools even run intensive courses to get you swimming quickly.

Choose Life

If you can swim already and want a new challenge, why not train to be a junior lifeguard? You learn about water safety, lifesaving, and how to deal with emergencies.

Keep Practicing

If you want to compete in swim meets, you'll have to practice hard, but it's well worth the effort! Training usually starts early in the morning, before the school day begins.

Dive In!

If you get a real buzz from diving, it's worth finding a coach to help you develop your technique. Always check that the water is deep enough to allow you to dive safely.

At Sea

If you swim in the ocean, make sure you go with an adult. There are currents and riptides that could carry even strong swimmers away from the shore. Look out for and obey warning flags, too—they are there to keep you safe.

Pool Party

There's so much fun to be had at your local swimming pool! Find out if your pool runs weekend kids' sessions, work out in a water aerobics class, or make up a synchronized swimming routine with your friends.

Outdoor Action

Playing sport in the open air works your muscles and gets your heart rate jumping! Winning is also a fab feeling, but nothing beats being part of a great team.

Soccer Sisters

Soccer is a very popular sport for girls and boys in the US and all over the world. So why not join your nearest soccer club? Be prepared to get muddy when you play!

Anyone for Tennis?

Tennis may not be an obvious team game, but if you join a tennis club, you'll make a lot of new friends. Doubles matches are always lots of fun—especially if it's a close game!

Old Favorites

Do you play softball, field hockey, or basketball at school? These are all terrific team sports. When you train, you'll learn tactics as well as improve your coordination and fitness.

Sophie's Annual Backyard Games

Starts 2:00p.m., next Saturday

Events:
limbo dancing

three-legged races

toss the boot

obstacle course

Medal Dreams

Can you run faster than your friends, jump higher, or throw a ball farther across the park? Athletics may be for you! Start training now for a gold medal at the next Olympics, or set up a mini-Games in your backyard.

On the Map

Orienteering is an outdoor activity that gives you plenty of fresh air and exercise. You and your buddies use a map and compass to find a set of marked spots, before racing back to base. Give it a go!

Work It Out

If sports are not your thing, don't say no to all outdoor exercise—just be creative about it! You could try setting up a treasure hunt so you and your friends can run around looking for clues.

Eat Smart

You're more likely to stay in shape and feel well if you have a nutritious diet. This means eating healthy meals, and saving candy and treats for special occasions.

Meal Deal

You may be a busy bee, but make time to eat three meals a day. Don't skip breakfast, or munch too much between meals. If you must have a snack, make a healthy choice.

Balancing Act

There are five key food groups. You should eat some food from each group during the day—a lot of 1 and 2, and only a little of 4.

1. bread and cereals
2. fruits and vegetables
3. dairy foods
4. sweet and fatty foods
5. meat, fish, and eggs

Five a Day

Fruits and vegetables are packed with vitamins and minerals, which all help your body to work properly. Make a real effort to eat five portions of fruit and vegetables every single day.

Eat Up!

Don't forget that smoothies and fruit juice count toward your five-a-day. Don't try to hide the salad and veggies on your plate— eat them all up, including the greens!

Dairy Foods

Creamy dairy foods like yogurt, milk, and cheese contain calcium—a mineral that helps your bones and teeth grow strong. Be dairy food-friendly and drink a glass of milk a day.

Feeling thirsty?

We all need to eat food, but water is even more important for our survival. You need to drink at least two to four pints of water a day—even more if the weather is hot.

Snack and Go

Next time you take a sack lunch to school or go on a picnic, stash some new things in your lunch box! There are all sorts of tasty dips, wraps, and snacks to try.

Wheat Is Sweet

Whole wheat bread is better for you than white bread, because it contains whole grains. Get used to eating your sandwiches on whole wheat—and try to eat the crusts, too!

Pack a Snack

Next time you're packing for a picnic, ask your mom or dad if you can leave any unhealthy stuff at home. Replace chips and chocolate with options like fruit, granola bars, and nuts.

D.I.Y. Nibbles

Ask if you can bake your own yummy treats. Granola, or oat, bars taste great and they are good for you, too! If you make too many to eat by yourself, take some into school to share with your friends. There's a tasty oat bar recipe on page 16.

Mix it Up

Always take a bottle of water out with you—it's important to top up your fluid levels throughout the day. If you're tired of plain tap water, add a splash of fruit juice to give it some flavor.

Plan Ahead

You'll soon get bored if you always eat the same thing. Experiment with different fillings for your sandwiches and wraps. Plan a week's lunches, so you eat something different every day.

This week's sandwiches:

Monday	cream cheese, ham, and cucumber
Tuesday	tuna crunch
Wednesday	hummus and shredded carrot
Thursday	chicken, raisins, and spinach
Friday	shrimp cocktail

Shopping List:
canned tuna
spinach leaves
sweet peppers
cream cheese
tortilla wraps

Get Involved

Make a list of the healthy snacks you would like to eat when you're on the go. Talk about the list with your mom and dad, then go grocery shopping together to buy the tasty things you have agreed on.

15

Let's Get Cooking

The best way to learn to cook is to get in the kitchen and help! Watch how your mom or dad prepares food, then pull on an apron and join in.

Baking Bars

Make a batch of fruity granola bars. These tasty snacks aren't just delicious—they're healthy, too!

Super-quick granola bars

You will need:
1/2 cup (125g) butter
1/2 cup (100g) light brown sugar
3 tbsp (60g) honey
3 cups (225g) rolled oats
3/4 cup (75g) dried fruit or nuts*

*Why not add dried raisins, apricots, coconut, or a mix of nuts and seeds?

1. Set the oven to 350°F/180°C/ gas mark 4.
2. Ask an adult to help you melt the butter, sugar, and honey in a nonstick pan.
3. Stir in the oats and dried fruit.
4. Scrape the mixture into a baking pan, then bake it for half an hour.
5. Take out, allow to cool, and cut into bars!

Cupcake Creations

For a special occasion, try baking some cupcakes. When they're cool, whip up some buttercream frosting, then decorate your frosted cup cakes with pretty sprinkles.

Make a Menu

When you've had some practice in the kitchen, try cooking a complete meal. Get together with a friend and plan an appetizer, entrée, and dessert. Keep things simple the first time around.

Take care in the kitchen. Always ask an adult to help you before cutting food or using the oven or stove.

Get Organized

Write a list of all the ingredients that you'll need for your meal. Go to the store to buy the stuff, then get cooking!

Dine in Style

To make your meal extra special, decorate the kitchen like a fancy restaurant, with flowers, napkins, and a tablecloth. Write out the menu so your guests know what dishes to look forward to!

Looking Good

It's important to try to look your best, because looking good also makes you feel great. Find your style and get ready to shine!

New Style

With long hair, there are all sorts of styles you can try out, but girls with short hair can have fun, too! If you have a shorter cut, jazz up your look with barettes, gels, and funky hair accessories.

Top Knots

Always brush your hair before you style it to pull out the tangles! Give boring old ponytails a makeover by twisting them into messy top knots. Try fixing a side knot, or even two high ones at the back.

Braid Trick

Wash your hair and tie it into a lot of little braids while it is damp. Let your hair dry naturally, then untie the braids. You'll be left with tumbling, wavy hair!

Fashion Exchange

If you're fed up with your wardrobe, don't wait until your next shopping trip. Ask your mom or dad, then revamp your style by trading clothes with your best friend.

Fashionista Closet Tips:

⭐ organize clothes by color

⭐ keep your shoes neatly in a rack

⭐ give to a thrift store anything you haven't worn for a year

⭐ pop a fragranced cushion in with socks, panty hose, and pjs

Makeovers and Makeup

It is fun to experiment with makeup, but try not to overdo it when you give your friend a makeover! Just a dab of lip gloss and a touch of blush will give her a lovely, natural look.

Attention to Detail

Looking good is all about the details. Pick accessories that make the most of your outfit. Break up boring tops with a funky belt or team with a sparkly necklace.

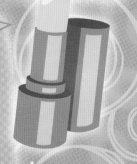

Perfectly Polished

Looking good isn't just about fashion—it's about taking care of your whole body, inside and out!

Choose Your Treats

Did you know that the good eating habits explained earlier can also affect your looks? If you want glowing skin and lovely hair, say "no" to junk food. When you are hungry, choose fruit instead of chips, and water instead of soda.

Wonderful Water

Your skin needs lots and lots of water! Drink plenty to keep it feeling soft. Wash your face with lukewarm water every morning and evening, using a clean towel to gently pat the skin dry.

Sun and Sleep

Your skin is precious, so look after it well. Get enough beauty sleep every night—if you don't feel fresh, your skin won't look fresh! In hot weather, use sunscreen and wear a sun hat to protect your skin.

Hair Food

A good diet will help keep your hair shiny and healthy, too. Foods like meat, fish, cheese, and eggs are full of protein—just the stuff for glossy, shiny hair.

Good Hair Day

Be kind to your hair! Brush it well every day, and have regular trims at the salon. This will stop you from getting split ends and keep your hair in top condition.

Salon Secrets

1. Wash your hair regularly.
2. Always rinse your locks after swimming.
3. When you wash your hair, let it dry naturally sometimes.
4. If you have to use a hairdryer, dry your hair with a towel first.
5. Don't brush your hair when it's wet or it might stretch and break.

Freshen Up

Do you like chilling out at the end of the day in a nice hot tub? Care for your body from top to toe and let your natural beauty shine through!

Smelly Stuff

Water is best for your skin when you bathe or shower—you don't need loads of soaps and products, however sweet they smell. Warm water will clean out tiny pores in your skin without blocking them up.

Sensitive Skin

If you are muddy after playing outside, then you'll need to use some soap to get the dirt off! If your skin is sensitive, choose a mild soap and don't use too much of it.

Break a Sweat

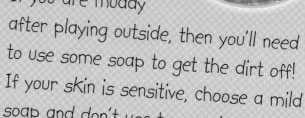

When you do something energetic, such as your favorite sport, you may get a bit sweaty. This doesn't have to be a problem—just put on some deodorant before you head out.

Handy Hygiene

It's important to wash your hands during the day, especially before you eat, after going to the bathroom, and when you've been playing with animals. Washing your hands stops germs from spreading.

Love Those Nails!

When you have a bath or shower, check your hands and clean your fingernails if you need to! Long, dirty fingernails don't look great, so try to file them so they stay neat.

Brush Up

No one likes bad breath, so make sure you don't have it. Brush your teeth every morning after breakfast, and every evening before bedtime. Have regular checkups at the dentist, too.

Prepare to Impress

Make time to get ready for special occasions.

- 1 hour before: take a bubble bath
- 45 minutes before: dry your hair
- 30 minutes before: get dressed
- 20 minutes before: style or pin up hair
- 10 minutes before: add a touch of makeup
- 5 minutes before: spritz on your favorite scent

Feeling Good

Feeling happy helps you stay healthy. Even when you're super-busy with school and friends, try to make time to de-stress and unwind.

Don't Worry!

Try not to worry too much. Worrying makes you sad and it can stop you sleeping well at night. When you're tired, you are more likely to catch a cold or get sick.

Talk About It

If something is bugging you, don't keep it a secret. Talking to someone will make you feel much better. Sharing a problem is the first step toward fixing it.

Get Some Help

If a problem won't go away, talk to an adult you trust, for example your teacher or someone in your family. If you are being bullied, this person will be able to help you get things straightened out.

Stop the Stress

If you are feeling stressed, stop what you are doing and do something else that you really enjoy. Take a walk, listen to some music, or play with your pet!

Wind Down

We all need plenty of sleep so that we can grow and function properly. If you find it hard to doze off at night, make sure you unwind before you go to bed.

Just Relax!

Some people relax best when they are with good friends. Others prefer to chill out on their own, perhaps reading quietly or listening to music. How do you relax?

Stress Busters!

take five deep breaths
call a caring friend
step into the sunshine
think of all your
favorite things
hug someone you love

Spoil Yourself

"Me time" matters! If you don't stop and spoil yourself sometimes, you'll end up feeling worn out and fed up.

Get Pampered

Make a date with your friends to have a girly pampering session. Try some new makeup, polish your nails, and do some homemade beauty treatments! Relax and have a fun time together.

Kayla is invited to Jenny's bedroom pampering session on Friday after school

Please bring your bathrobe and a hairbrush

RSVP (No little brothers allowed!)

Cool as a Cucumber

After a long day at school, lie on the couch and shut your eyes. Rest a thin slice of cucumber on each eyelid—it's a great way to soothe and refresh your tired eyes.

Shop Till You Drop

If you really need cheering up, the only answer may be to hit the mall with a friend. Treat yourselves to a cupcake in a café, then blow your allowance on something you've had your eye on for ages!

Happy Faces

Give your best buddy a facial massage. Smooth her forehead and cheeks with your fingertips, working in small circles. Be very gentle and try not to tickle!

Smells Good

Are you bored with the perfume you got last birthday? Have a scent-swapping party—the best part is trying out the fragrances and deciding which one you like best!

One-on-One

Ask your mom or dad to take you out somewhere, just the two of you. It doesn't have to be an expensive trip—you'll have fun being together and doing something different.

27

Sleep Tight

Everyone needs to sleep—even dynamic divas like you! Your body is growing, and that uses up loads of essential energy.

A Good Night's Sleep

If you don't get enough sleep, you can become tired and grouchy. You might also find it difficult to work properly at school. You need around ten hours of sleep a night to stay healthy and happy.

Early to Bed

It sounds obvious, but the easiest way to get more sleep is to go to bed earlier! On school days, try to be an early bird, saving your late nights for the weekend.

Calm Down

Choose to do calming things just before bedtime. Have a nice bath, and some warm milk. Don't do anything that makes your brain or body have to work too hard!

One Last Thing

Sometimes it's hard to get to sleep, but there can be good reasons for this. Give yourself time to wind down before you go to bed—don't play computer games or watch loud TV shows just before you switch off the light.

Bedtime Story

Try to get into the habit of reading a relaxing book at bedtime. It can be a novel, short story, or even one of your school subjects! You could listen to a "talking book" CD. You'll soon feel sleepy and ready to doze off.

Off to Sleep

If you really can't get to sleep, stop worrying. That will only keep you awake longer. Instead, think about something completely different—like an A to Z list of all your favorite celebs!

Dreamer's Dictionary

chocolate   time for a treat
forest   think something through
letter   listen to your heart
party   be more sociable
tunnel   keep moving forward

Happy and Healthy Quiz

Are you healthy inside and out? Get a notebook and write down the answers to this great lifestyle quiz.

 1. What's the healthiest way to get to school?
- **a** share a ride
- **b** walk or cycle
- **c** take the bus

 2. Which of these indoor sports will teach you to be fit and safe?
- **a** judo
- **b** chess
- **c** gymnastics

3. What's the best way to get into a new sport?
- **a** watch people playing it on TV
- **b** wait until a friend is interested in giving it a go
- **c** sign yourself up at your neighborhood sports club

4. In which sport can you play doubles matches?
- **a** tennis
- **b** hockey
- **c** basketball

5. Which of these meals is it OK to miss?
- **a** breakfast
- **b** any meal, if you don't feel like it
- **c** you should never miss a meal

6. Which of these helps your skin?

  a soda

  b junk food

  c water

7. If you're stressed, what's a good way to unwind?

  a play a computer game

  b take a long walk

  c eat a takeout

8. How much sleep do you really need?

  a as little as you can get away with

  b about six hours a night

  c about ten hours a night

Look back at these pages: *Get In Shape!* (pages 4-5); *Indoor Play* (pages 6-7); *Outdoor Action* (pages 10-11); *Eat Smart* (pages 12-13); *Perfectly Polished* (pages 20-21); *Feeling Good* (pages 24-25); *Sleep Tight* (pages 28-29).

How Well Did You Do?

Count your correct answers below to find out!

0-3   You're on the right track, but there's a lot more you can learn about how to stay happy and healthy.

4-6   Not bad! You've got a pretty clear idea of what's good for you and what isn't! Keep up the great work.

7-8   You're the best! You know just what to do to make sure you always look and feel amazing.

Quiz answers: 1. b, 2. a, 3. c, 4. a, 5. c, 6. c, 7. b, 8. c

Index